WHERE ARE THE MEN OF THE HOUR?

&

THE FAMILY

THE STRENGTH OF A NATION IS THE FAMILY, IF STRONG, YOUR NATION WILL BE STRONG

John A. Alexander

To learn more about John's work, upcoming releases, and exclusive updates, please visit:
www.bestsellersbyjohnaalexander.com

For direct contact:
author@bestsellersbyjohnaalexander.com

Published by

Ultra Publishers
www.ultrapublishers.com

Printed in the United States of America

Dedication

I dedicate this book to the men of today, fathers, sons, husbands, and leaders. The strength of a nation lies in the strength of its families. The attack is against men; if men are taken out, families can be destroyed. When men are absent, children suffer and grow up without the love and guidance of a father.

I believe that every man carries within him the potential to become the man God intended him to be. Please do not reject the importance of teaming up with God. Rejecting God's help means rejecting not only your future but the future of your family as well. I do not write for you to become a preacher, but to be the best father you can be so that your children may be proud of you. I also write for you to be the best husband, so you can pass on a template to your children of what it means to be not only the head of your home, but also its leader, provider, guide, and protector.

You might say, "You don't know my past, my hurts, or my upbringing." While I may not know your past, I also have mine. I was sexually abused at the age of seven and grew up without a father. I saw him only twice a year, and later in life, he reentered our lives. I got involved with the wrong crowd and lived a worldly life—perhaps one day, I'll share more details about it. I also had to witness both of my parents in different relationships.

So when it comes to hurts and trauma, I've had my share. That's why I'm not ashamed to talk about God and how He healed me. The God of the Bible came into my life and began the healing process, mending those wounds, those hurts, and teaching me to forgive. Even to this day, God is still working in my life.

I should be six feet under, but I am alive today because of what God did for me and my family. I am now a father to three wonderful boys and a husband to an amazing wife. Instead of walking away, she stayed and helped me through the process. If anyone paid a price, it was her, and I owe my life to both God and her. I now understand the pain I caused her and my family during my healing journey. So, men, there is hope for you. What God has done for others, He will do for you.

Even if you haven't experienced the past I had, this book can still minister to you in the areas of your life. We may not have arrived yet, but we can certainly improve our lives and become better individuals and better men.

The hardest thing for me was to become the men I ought be be for my family, my past crippled me in many ways and brought a lot of shame, I wanted my family to be proud of me , instead even though I had some victories I became my worse enemy and they had to suffer for it. Today I'm NOT the men I used to be and they see that in my life.

I pray this book speaks to you in a meaningful way and that you find answers and the miracles you need for yourself and your family.

"THE STRENGTH OF A NATION IS STRONG FAMILIES."

Acknowledgment

I am deeply grateful to God and my wonderful family for allowing me to gain the necessary experience to write this book. I have learned so much from them, through their acceptance, their forgiveness when I failed them, and their grace to stay by my side as I grew into a secure person.

I am also thankful for all those who have been part of my journey, too many to mention. Thank you to each and every one of you; your love and prayers made all the difference in my life and gave me the strength to continue moving toward my miracle.

May God bless them and meet their needs as they met mine during my healing process.

I believe in being transparent in my writing because "TRUTH WITH EXPERIENCE IS MORE POWERFUL THAN TRUTH ALONE." Sharing both my defeats and victories is what I believe will help someone out there.

About the Author

John has traveled extensively around the world, teaching and speaking to companies and religious organizations on topics that remain deeply relevant today. His lectures span a wide range of subjects—from business and politics to personal development, sales, leadership, and marriage—all with a consistent purpose: to challenge his audience to think critically, grow confidently, and strive to become better individuals in every area of life.

With more than forty years of experience influencing and inspiring people face-to-face, John is now embracing a lifelong passion—writing. Through his books, he seeks to share the lessons, insights, and wisdom he has gained over decades of teaching, leadership, and global experience.

He plans to publish four to five books each year, ensuring this is only the beginning of what readers can expect from him. John's knowledge is profound, thought-provoking, and always grounded in truth.

Table of Contents

PART 1

PART 2

PART 1

INTRODUCTION

This book comes out of years of observing how the world has changed and how families are desperately struggling, affecting our children and the next generation.

I have seen how, in many cases, fathers have lost their way and are no longer fulfilling their role as the head of their homes. They are not the fathers they ought to be, the protectors and the providers. Of course, this is not true of every father, but it happens far too often.

This book is written to challenge fathers and give families something to reflect on. If even one reader is convinced and takes the initiative to fix what needs fixing, we will see stronger homes and stronger families.

I write from areas I have researched, **but mostly from personal experience.** I write about what I have lived through, my failures and my victories, and how I found a path to become a better husband, a better father, and a better individual who can contribute to society and help create a better world for our children.

Whether you are in your twenties or your sixties, we must aim to do what we perhaps should have done years ago. We must fight for our homes and for our loved ones.

The strength of a nation is the family

Nehemiah 4:14, King James Version

*And I looked, and rose up, and said unto the nobles, and to the rulers, and to the rest of the people, Be not ye afraid of them. Remember the Lord, which is great and terrible, **and fight for your brethren, your sons, and your daughters, your wives, and your houses.***

CHAPTER ONE: WHERE ARE YOU, ADAM?

The Temptation and Fall of Man

Genesis 3:1–9, New King James Version

In this portion of Scripture, we see something very important that we must understand.

The serpent entices the woman to eat from the forbidden tree. When she eats, nothing appears to happen immediately. However, the moment she gives fruit to her husband, the curse takes effect. Separation from God begins, sin enters humanity, and sin becomes the destroyer of individuals, homes, and families.

In verse 9, when God speaks, He does not call to the woman. He calls to the man and says, **"Where are you, Adam?"**

This question forms the foundation of this book. That same voice still speaks today.

God is still asking,

Where are you, men?

Where are you, fathers?

Where are you, husbands?

The battle today is directed toward men, toward fathers, toward providers, toward those called to protect their homes and families.

What do we see around us?

We see families without fathers in the home.

We see absent fathers and children longing for their love and presence.

We see prisons filled with individuals who grew up in broken homes, often with only one parent present, and sometimes with neither parent present at all.

These broken structures leave deep wounds in sons and daughters.

We must rise up and do everything we can to become the men we are called to be. Whether single or married, we must break free from cultural norms and fulfill the God-given responsibility **to become the men of the hour.**

My hope is that something in this book will awaken you, stir you, and move you to fight for your home and your family.

CHAPTER TWO: TO THE SINGLE MAN

One of my greatest regrets in life, and I am sure many others share this feeling, is the number of years wasted without a clear purpose or direction. We often fail to realize that whatever we sow, we will eventually reap.

What do I regret most?

Education.

If I had been able to look into my future and understand how important education truly is, I might have pursued a degree or developed a specialized skill. While education is not everything, it could have provided stability, opened doors, and secured my future more effectively.

Instead, I worked various temporary jobs, mainly in sales, and eventually became skilled in marketing and communication. **Yet I often wonder how different life might have been with stronger preparation earlier.**

My encouragement to single men is simple: Stop wasting time on things that do not benefit your present or your future.

What does wasted time look like?

Spending weekends going out, spending money, and starting each Monday broke.

Rewarding yourself without first living a productive week.

Weekends should be a reward for meaningful progress made during the week. If the week has not been productive, the priority should be preparation, planning, and discipline for what lies ahead.

There is a well-known truth:

We do not plan to fail. We fail to plan.

For many years, I depended only on my potential. I believed I could always recover from mistakes. Instead of using my energy to research, study, and build a secure future, I worked against myself.

Imagine directing that same energy toward discovering a career path, building stability, and creating long-term success. Life would produce many more meaningful rewards.

A lesson from one of my boys

My youngest son, at twenty-one, discovered an opportunity that allowed him to earn money and become successful. What surprised me most was not his success, but his discipline.

Instead of celebrating every weekend like many young men, he began removing negative influences from his life. He understood that achieving his goals required focus, sacrifice, and wise relationships. I'm grateful to have three boys who think alike, choosing the right path and avoiding toxic relationships that can pull them away from their potential. I'm so proud of them and what they have become.

I often see the opposite. Some young men succeed financially but spend everything trying to impress others. This attracts people who benefit from them without sharing their vision.

If you remove those influences and surround yourself with people who pursue purpose, discipline, and growth, you will find:

- Potential mentors
- True friends
- Relationships built on shared direction

As the saying goes:

If you want to cross the bridge, you must ask someone who has already crossed it.

Distractions and relationships

Life contains many distractions that steal time and delay purpose:

- Constant job changes without direction
- Pursuing unhealthy romantic relationships
- Emotional wounds that require time to heal

There is nothing wrong with relationships. However, wisdom says:

- Make friends.
- Make best friends.
- Then marry a best friend.

Choose someone who supports your goals, strengthens your faith, and builds your future rather than weakening it.

Becoming a great husband and father begins during singleness, not after marriage.

My beginning may differ from yours, but the lessons remain the same.

CHAPTER THREE: MY UPBRINGING

I believe many of our deepest struggles are connected to how we were raised. Our childhood experiences shape our thinking, relationships, and emotional responses far into adulthood.

To help you understand this truth, I must begin with my own story.

When I was about six years old, I was sexually abused by a man after a basketball practice.

This raises painful but necessary questions:

Does childhood trauma affect future relationships?

Does it influence marriage, trust, and emotional health?

Research strongly suggests that it does.

Studies across North America indicate:

Approximately 1 in 6 boys experience sexual abuse before age eighteen.

Nearly one in four men experiences some form of sexual contact violence in their lifetime.

90 to 95 percent of male sexual abuse cases are never reported.

Many survivors wait over fifteen years before telling anyone.

These numbers reveal a hidden crisis affecting countless men, families, and future generations.

Long-term effects on men

Male survivors often experience:

- Emotional and psychological struggles
- Depression, anxiety, and post-traumatic stress
- Shame, guilt, and feelings of being damaged
- Suicidal thoughts or self-harm
- Emotional numbness or dissociation
- Relational and behavioral challenges
- Difficulty trusting others
- Sexual confusion or dysfunction
- Substance abuse
- Anger or aggression
- Physical health consequences
- Chronic illness and pain
- Fatigue and stress-related conditions

Social expectations often silence men. Many are taught to appear strong and unemotional, making disclosure extremely difficult.

Yet recovery is possible through:

- Counseling and trauma-focused therapy
- Support networks with other survivors
- Healthy activities, relationships, **and faith**

My personal journey

These realities affected my own life and relationships.

I did not speak about my abuse publicly until I was forty-five years old, while teaching before a crowd that included my family. They were unprepared to hear it, yet speaking the truth began a process of healing, not only for me but for others with similar stories.

Another major wound came from my parents' separation. My father moved to another country, and I saw him only a few times each year. Although we later restored our relationship, the absence left deep emotional marks.

I also witnessed both of my parents in relationships with other partners after their separation. As a young child, seeing my mother with another man created confusion, jealousy, and mistrust that later damaged my own relationships and marriage.

For years I carried:

- Jealousy
- Insecurity
- Emotional distance
- Self-centered behavior

Through counseling and faith, God began transforming my life. I slowly became:

- A better husband
- A better father
- A more secure individual

And this is my prayer for every reader:

There is light at the end of the tunnel.

There is hope.

The Creator who formed you is able to heal you.

CHAPTER FOUR: AFTER MY ABUSE

After the abuse I experienced as a child, I had to live with its effects and consequences.

Looking back now, I can see more clearly what happened inside me. My desire in sharing this is not to expose pain, but to help you, the reader, find healing rather than continue hiding your hurt.

The effect

I created a hidden room in the basement of my heart and locked those memories away, determined never to revisit them.

Did I do this intentionally? **No.**

I simply shut down emotionally and became what many would call emotionally avoidant. As a child, I did not have the ability to process what I had seen or experienced. I carried the pain of abuse and the confusion of my family situation silently.

To survive, I developed a personality that functioned well in public. I could speak to crowds, communicate confidently, and succeed in sales and marketing. People praised my abilities, and that public success allowed me to function for many years.

But God eventually revealed something to me.

He showed me that the basement room of my heart had to be opened and healed.

The mistake of survival

I tried to bring my public personality into my home and family life. That could never work, because it was not the real me.

My family did not need a performer.

They needed a secure, loving, emotionally present husband and father.

By the grace of God, my eyes were opened. **I began to understand the pain my wife had carried for years**. She saw what I could not see. She saw a wounded child living inside an adult man.

For the first time in my life, I began to feel real emotions. I saw how I had hurt my family, and I also saw their incredible love and patience toward me.

Instead of abandoning me, they waited for my healing.

I shifted my priorities. My public life became secondary. **My family became primary.** It felt like learning to walk again. Freedom slowly replaced emotional numbness. **Avoidance was replaced with the courage to confront the past.**

Today, my goal is to help others open their own hidden rooms and walk toward freedom. If this book helps even one

father become who God intended him to be, it will have fulfilled
its purpose.

13

CHAPTER FIVE: MISSING MEN, MISSING FATHERS

Watching parents separate can deeply wound a child. It certainly wounded me.

That is why I urge every parent to fight for their marriage, their children, and their home. **The strength of a nation is the family**. When families break, nations weaken, and children search for love in dangerous places.

Children often feel forced to choose sides during separation or divorce. Some grow to resent one parent while protecting the other. None of this is what children truly want. They simply want both parents to be whole and present.

There is a spiritual battle against the family.

We see the results everywhere:

- Addiction
- Crime
- Broken relationships
- Anger and hopelessness

Many parents later live with deep regret over what might have been different.

But healing is possible. When you find healing, you can help others find it too. **A better world truly begins with one healed life at a time.**

A father's responsibility

Faith in God became my foundation. **If God created us, then only the Creator fully knows how to heal us.** Looking back, I recognize what I would tell fathers today:

The old me

I spent little quality time with my sons. Even physically present, my mind was elsewhere.

The new me

I invested deeply in relationships and connection. I learned to listen, to care about their interests, and to be emotionally present.

One of my sons once said, half joking, "Dad, I think we are spending too much time together."

To me, that was evidence of healing.

I also had to apologize to my older sons for my earlier absence. Healing sometimes begins with humility.

Today, I pray for my children daily and strive to live rightly before God so my prayers will carry spiritual weight.

Scripture teaches:

The effective, fervent prayer of a righteous man avails much.
James 5:16

Righteousness means being in right standing with God. That is the only place from which true spiritual authority flows.

Treating your wife as a queen

Many men want to be kings in their homes. **But a true king first learns to treat his wife as a queen.**

Scripture says an excellent wife is the crown of her husband. If the crown is damaged, the king must examine how he has cared for it. Women often respond to how they are treated. Honor produces honor. Love produces love.

CHAPTER SIX: THE UMBRELLA OF YOUR HOME

I believe fathers carry delegated authority from God. Scripture calls the man the head of the home, and God also provides the wisdom needed for that responsibility. Being an effective father requires selflessness. We must care more about our family than ourselves.

When we do, God often provides supernatural help, strength, and insight.

Protection and discernment

There were moments in my life when I sensed God's guidance in protecting my children. **Experiences like these taught me the seriousness of a father's role.**

We must remain spiritually attentive, emotionally present, and honest in our guidance.

Sometimes that guidance includes prayerful patience.

I remember praying persistently about one of my son's relationships until God brought clarity and resolution.

Understanding development

Research shows the human brain continues developing into the mid-twenties and sometimes beyond. This reminds parents to practice patience, wisdom, and steady guidance during those formative years.

The umbrella illustration

A father is like an umbrella over his home. **If the umbrella has holes, harm can enter. If the umbrella is whole, protection remains.** That is why Scripture calls men to fight for their families. Even in single-parent homes, God becomes the protector and provider for those who trust Him. **No matter the past, a parent can rise again and become a hero to their children.**

CHAPTER SEVEN: MENTAL CHALLENGES AND FINDING PURPOSE

This chapter is deeply personal.

Mental illness is affecting millions of families across Canada and the United States. Roughly one in five adults experiences mental health challenges each year, and many begin in childhood or adolescence.

I share this not as a doctor, but as a father who fought for one of my sons.

My son's struggle

My firstborn was diagnosed with ADHD at an early age. Over time, his condition worsened and was eventually diagnosed as schizophrenia. Those years were the hardest of my life. I took him to hospitals, programs, and specialists. At times he could barely communicate. Safety often required hospitalization. Yet I refused to give up.

Prayer became my lifeline.

Eventually we found a place that helped him recognize his condition and begin real healing. Slowly, stability returned.

The miracle of perseverance

Today, in 2026, my son is living with remarkable improvement:

- Stable health
- Employment
- Responsibility
- Active faith

For families still in the struggle, my heart is with you.

Do not give up.

Fathers must fight for their families even when the battle lasts years.

Quitting brings regret.

Perseverance can reveal miracles.

Scripture reminds us:

*Let us not grow weary while doing good, for in due season we shall **reap if we do not lose heart.*** Galatians 6:9

CHAPTER EIGHT: STEPS TO BECOMING THE MAN GOD WANTS YOU TO BECOME

The Strength to Kneel: Surrender as the Beginning of Manhood

There is a version of manhood that is loud, forceful, and allergic to weakness. It dominates conversations, chases status, and protects its image at all costs. Yet beneath the surface, it is often fragile, easily threatened, easily angered, and easily shaken.

Scripture presents a very different picture.

The first defining act of true masculine strength is not conquest. **It is surrender.**

In Luke 22:42, on the night before the crucifixion, Jesus prays, *"Father, if You are willing, take this cup from Me; nevertheless not My will, but Yours be done."*

In that moment we see the clearest image of manhood ever lived. Not because He overpowered Rome. Not because He commanded angels. **But because He submitted His will to the Father when it cost Him everything.**

The world says, "Real men take control."

Christ shows us, "Real men submit to God."

The First Failure of Manhood

To understand surrender, we must return to the beginning.

In Genesis 3, Adam stands in the garden with purpose, provision, and fellowship with God. Yet when temptation comes, he chooses autonomy over obedience.

The root sin is not only disobedience. It is self-rule.

"I will decide."

"I will define."

"I will determine what is good."

That instinct still lives in every man.

Biblical manhood begins where Adam failed: **in surrender.**

Why Surrender Feels Like Weakness

Many men resist surrender because it sounds passive. But surrender to God is not resignation. It is active trust. It takes greater strength to lay down your will than to assert it. Anyone can react in anger. Anyone can chase impulse. Anyone can protect ego. But to restrain yourself out of reverence for God, that is strength under control. The strongest man in history knelt.

The Daily Battle for the Throne

Surrender is not a one-time decision. It is a daily dethroning of self. Every morning a question rises:

Who will rule today? Your emotions? Your ambition? Your appetites? Or God?

Partial surrender is still resistance.

To become the man God intends, every area must be yielded:

- Sexuality
- Finances
- Speech
- Thoughts
- Ambitions
- Relationships

Not because God seeks control, but because He is forming you into something greater than your impulses could ever build.

Surrender Restores Order

When men refuse surrender:

- Authority becomes domination
- Strength becomes intimidation
- Desire becomes addiction
- Leadership becomes selfishness

But under God's authority:

- Strength becomes service
- Ambition becomes stewardship

- Power becomes protection
- Influence becomes responsibility

You do not lose masculinity in surrender. **You redeem it.**

Identity, Power, and Peace

Many men cling to control because they believe their worth depends on performance. But Scripture teaches identity is rooted in being a child of God, not in achievement.

When identity is secure:

- You do not need to prove yourself
- You do not need to dominate
- You do not need to win every argument
- You do not need to protect your ego

The surrendered man gains:

- Clarity of purpose
- Inner peace
- Moral authority
- Emotional stability

Not because life becomes easier, **but because the foundation becomes stronger.**

Surrender in Marriage and Fatherhood

A wife does not need a flawless man. She needs a surrendered one.

A husband who bows to God:

- Apologizes quickly
- Leads gently
- Protects faithfully
- Loves sacrificially

Children learn more from a father's surrender than from his words.

Authority without surrender becomes harsh.

Authority with surrender becomes safe.

The Courage to Yield

- It takes courage to confess sin.
- It takes courage to walk away from temptation.
- It takes courage to trust God with the future.

In one garden, Adam grasped and fell. In another garden, Jesus yielded and overcame. Your manhood will follow one of those patterns.

A Prayer of Surrender

"Father, I release control. My plans, my pride, and my desires I lay before You. Shape me, correct me, and lead me. I trust Your will above my own."

The man who kneels before God will stand strong before the pressures of the world.

CHAPTER NINE: LIVING IN RIGHT, STANDING WITH GOD

Every man eventually discovers a powerful truth:

Life does not work correctly when God is absent from the center.

We may achieve success, recognition, or wealth, yet still feel empty, restless, or burdened with regret.

Right standing with God restores what success alone cannot give:

- Peace in the heart
- Direction for the future
- Strength for responsibility
- Hope beyond failure

Jeremiah 29:11 reminds us that God's thoughts toward us are thoughts of peace and hope, not destruction.

God sees the end from the beginning.

He knows every failure, every wound, and every possibility for redemption.

Daily Positioning Before God

Spiritual strength does not happen accidentally. It is built through daily surrender, prayer, repentance, and obedience. Each morning becomes an opportunity to realign the heart with God's will.

Confession removes pride.

Prayer invites strength.

Scripture renews the mind.

Obedience releases peace.

A man who walks daily with God develops:

- Stability in crisis
- Wisdom in decisions
- Patience in trials
- Compassion in leadership

This is not religious performance. It is relational transformation.

Praying for Family and Future

A father's prayers carry spiritual influence. When a man lives in right standing with God, his prayers protect:

- His marriage
- His children

- His home

- His future generations

Faithfulness in private produces strength in public.

The goal is not perfection.

The goal is surrender and consistency.

CHAPTER TEN: BECOMING THE SINGLE MAN GOD WANTS YOU TO BE

The Purpose of Singleness

Singleness is not an accident, a mistake, or a punishment. **It is preparation.** Many people treat singleness like a waiting room for life to begin. But in God's design, it is a training ground where character is formed before covenant is given.

God shapes one life before joining two lives.

The real question is not, "Why am I still single?"

The real question is, "What is God forming in me during this season?"

Singleness as Preparation

Throughout Scripture, preparation always comes before promotion.

If we rush into relationships without character, we enter marriage unprepared to sustain it.

Marriage does not fix loneliness.

Marriage reveals character.

You must become whole in Christ before building life with another person.

Waiting is not punishment.

Waiting is protection.

Redeeming Time

The greatest danger in singleness is not loneliness. It is wasted time.

Time is one of God's most valuable gifts. Once lost, it never returns.

Singleness provides opportunity to:

- Grow spiritually
- Build discipline
- Develop education and skills
- Plan financially
- Discover calling

Prayer and preparation must walk together.

God blesses diligence and responsibility.

The future is built in the hidden decisions of today.

Avoiding Distractions

Distractions quietly steal destiny:

- Endless entertainment

- Lack of direction
- Misused energy

Wise singles ask, "Is this helping me become who God is calling me to be?"

If the answer is no, change direction.

Choosing Friends and Relationships Wisely

Friends will either **strengthen faith and discipline or normalize compromise and laziness.**

Choose relationships that pursue God, purpose, truth, and integrity. The same wisdom applies to romantic relationships.

A future spouse should share:

- Christian convictions
- Commitment to purity
- Spiritual maturity
- Vision for family and calling

Physical attraction may begin a relationship. Spiritual unity sustains it.

Living With Purpose Today

Your future is not decided someday. It is shaped daily. Every habit matters. Every decision matters. Every hour matters. Singleness is not the season to drift. It is the season to build:

- Faith

- Character

- Wisdom

- Readiness for God's future

When you redeem this season well, you will step into the future with confidence, strength, and peace rather than regret.

CONCLUSION

The Call Still Stands

The question God asked in the garden still echoes through every generation:

"Where are you?"

Not as a voice of condemnation, but as a call to return. A call to rise. A call to become the man you were created to be.

This book has spoken about pain, failure, healing, fatherhood, surrender, and purpose. If there is one truth that remains above all others, it is this:

Your past does not have the final word. God does.

No matter what you have faced, no matter what you have lost, no matter how far you feel from the man you should be, there is still time to stand, to fight, and to rebuild.

Strong families begin with surrendered men.

Healed fathers raise secure children.

Faithful husbands create peaceful homes.

And restored homes shape the future of nations.

The world does not simply need stronger men. **It needs transformed men.** Men who kneel before God so they can stand with courage in life. Men who choose responsibility over escape. **Men who fight for their wives, their children, and their calling.**

The call is not only for someone else. It is for you. And the moment to answer is not someday. It is today.

So rise with faith.

Lead with humility.

Love with sacrifice.

Stand with courage.

And may your life become proof that when a man surrenders fully to God, generations can change forever.

Here's was my turning point at the age of 23 years old, this is when I turned my will to Gods will. You are welcome to pray it if you like, what happened to me it can happen for you, God wants the best for all those that surrender to Him.

Pray with me…

"Dear God I know I'm a sinner and I need forgiveness, I believe that Jesus Christ died on the cross for all my sins, please forgive me and I'm willing to follow you as the Lord of my life , help me to be the men I ought to be, the father I need to be and the best in every area of my life I pray as I surrender to you, in your name I pray, Amen."

PART 2

CHAPTER ONE: THE STRENGTH OF A NATION BEGINS AT HOME

I had just returned from a beautiful weekend with my lovely wife and one of my boys. It was one of those rare moments where everything felt right. We laughed, we talked, we shared meals, we enjoyed each other's presence, and my heart was full. As much as I wished my other boys were there with us, I could see the joy in my wife's face, and I could see my youngest son genuinely happy. For a moment, everything was peaceful.

But in the middle of all that joy, the Lord spoke to my heart.

Not with thunder.

Not with fear.

But with a deep, gentle conviction:

"Many families are losing what I have given them."

And what is that?

The gift of a family.

We live in a world where people celebrate success, fame, money, political power, and accomplishments, yet the very foundation God gave humanity is being neglected: the home. The Lord began to impress on me something powerful: the strength of a nation is measured by the strength of its families. And that is exactly why the enemy is attacking our homes with such force today.

- Broken marriages.
- Rebellious children.
- Homes without prayer.
- Financial stress.
- Addictions.
- Divorce.
- Fathers absent.
- Mothers overwhelmed.
- Children lost and confused.
- Young people running from the very protection God placed over them.

Some parents no longer know where their children even are.

And while nations argue about politics, economies, and world events… the real battlefield is not in Washington, Ottawa, or the UN.

The real battlefield is the home.

A Nation Is Only As Strong As Its Families

No government can legislate family unity.

No president can rebuild your marriage.

No school system can raise your children for you.

No society can teach your home how to love God.

The future of a nation is shaped in living rooms, at dinner tables, during bedtime prayers, in marriages, and through the daily example parents give their children.

You want to save a nation?

Strengthen the home.

You want to change society?

Restore the family.

You want revival?

Start in the living room, not the stadium.

Scripture confirms this over and over:

~Husbands, love your wives as Christ loved the church… (Ephesians 5:25)

~Wives, respect your husbands… (1 Peter 3:7)

~Train up a child in the way he should go… (Proverbs 22:6)

~Forgive one another as the Lord forgave you… (Colossians 3:13)

THE FAMILY IS GOD'S FIRST INSTITUTION

Before God created the church…

Before He gave commandments…

Before He established governments…

Before nations even existed…

God created a family.

Adam and Eve. Husband and wife. Father and mother.

The family was , and still is ,God's master plan for building strong societies.

When the family collapses, society collapses.

When the home breaks, the nation breaks.

When children are unprotected, the future is unprotected.

Satan knows this too well. That is why his first attack wasn't on the angels or the structures of the earth. His first attack was on a family.

My Message to Every Family

I speak not only as a teacher or a preacher…

I speak as a father.

A husband.

A man who has made mistakes and still learning from them.

A man who lost time with his first two boys but fought to restore what the enemy tried to steal.

It is never too late to rebuild your home.

It is never too late to strengthen your family.

It is never too late to put God back at the center.

We can build nations again — one family at a time.

Strong families produce strong communities.

Strong communities produce strong churches.

Strong churches produce strong nations.

If we can restore the home… we can restore the nation.

CHAPTER TWO: GOD'S DESIGN FOR MARRIAGE—LOVE, HONOR & SACRIFICE

Marriage is not a human invention. It is not a government contract. It is not a cultural tradition. God Himself created marriage, and because He created it, **only God has the authority to define it.**

Strong marriages build strong families. Strong families build strong nations.

THE HUSBAND'S CALLING: LOVE LIKE CHRIST LOVED THE CHURCH

"Husbands, love your wives as Christ loved the church and gave Himself for her." — Ephesians 5:25

This is sacrificial love — protecting, leading, serving, forgiving, and valuing your wife above yourself.

THE WIFE'S CALLING: HONOR, RESPECT & PARTNERSHIP

"Wives, submit to your husbands as unto the Lord." 1 Peter 3:7

Biblical submission is honor and unity. A wife brings wisdom, strength, and spiritual discernment to the home.

MARRIAGE IS NOT 50/50, IT IS 100/100

A godly marriage requires full commitment, faithfulness, and teamwork. Marriage is a covenant, not a contract.

A MARRIAGE WITHOUT GOD CANNOT WITHSTAND STORMS.

Homes built on Christ stand firm. Homes built on pride or emotions collapse. **God restores broken marriages when couples surrender to Him.**

YOUR MARRIAGE PREACHES TO YOUR CHILDREN

Children learn love, communication, forgiveness, and values by watching their parents. A strong marriage gives children emotional security. Parents give their children a template so they can follow it in the future to have successful relationships and a God-given marriage.

THE ENEMY TARGETS MARRIAGES

If Satan destroys the marriage, he weakens the children, the future, and the nation. **But a marriage built on God destroys the enemy's plans.**

YOUR MARRIAGE IS A MINISTRY

Before you lead or serve, your marriage is your first ministry. A godly marriage is a testimony and a lighthouse.

A PRAYER FOR MARRIAGES

"Lord, restore marriages that are hurting. Teach husbands to love like Christ and wives to honor in unity. Strengthen every couple reading this, and let their marriage reflect Your glory. In your name we pray, Amen."

CHAPTER THREE: RAISING GODLY CHILDREN IN A GODLESS WORLD

There has never been a generation of children more attacked, more confused, more pressured, and more spiritually targeted than the generation growing up today. Children who once grew up with innocence now face battles that previous generations never imagined.

Proverbs 22:6 teaches us: *"Train up a child in the way he should go, and when he is old, he will not depart from it."* Raising a child gives them a home. Training a child gives them a future.

CHILDREN NEED MORE THAN HOMES — THEY NEED DIRECTION

Today, many children lack boundaries, discipline, spiritual teaching, and moral guidance. Parents are the protectors of the home. They are the spiritual guardians God uses to shape the next generation.

YOUR CHILDREN NEED YOU MORE THAN THEY NEED THE WORLD

When parents are too busy, the world steps in. Culture, media, and peers become the voices shaping children. But children need parents who pray, love, teach, correct, and model godly characters.

DISCIPLINE IS LOVE

Godly discipline guides, protects, and builds character. Discipline without love is abuse. Love without discipline is neglect. Parenting requires both.

THE POWER OF A PARENT'S EXAMPLE

Children imitate what they see. If they see prayer, forgiveness, respect, and faith, they learn it. Your example becomes their foundation.

WHEN CHILDREN LEAVE THEIR COVERING

Many children run from home too early, leaving the spiritual covering God designed to protect them. This exposes them to destructive influences. Parents must pray, guide, and fight for their children's hearts.

A GODLY CHILDHOOD BECOMES A GODLY ADULTHOOD

A child trained in God's ways becomes an adult of integrity, wisdom, and purpose. Raising godly children is not just parenting—it is nation-building.

A PRAYER FOR PARENTS

"Lord, strengthen every parent. Restore broken relationships, heal wounded hearts, and bring prodigals home. Raise a generation of God-fearing sons and daughters who walk in Your truth. Amen."

CHAPTER FOUR: THE ENEMY OF THE FAMILY—HOW SATAN ATTACKS THE HOME

The strength of a nation is rooted in the strength of its families, which is why Satan directs his fiercest attacks at the home. Destroy the family, and you weaken the future; break the home, and you cripple the nation. That is why the first part of this family manual starts with the head of the home: if the enemy destroys the head, he can destroy the family, but if the head is in place, no enemy will be able to defeat him or destroy his family. Men, wake up and be the father, husband, son, brother, and individual God wants you to be.

THE FIRST ATTACK IN HISTORY WAS AGAINST A FAMILY

Before Satan attacked cities or nations, he attacked a marriage—Adam and Eve. He targeted their unity, communication, trust, and obedience. **His strategy has never changed.**

HOW SATAN ATTACKS THE MODERN FAMILY

1. DIVISION IN MARRIAGE

Arguments, bitterness, pride, and unforgiveness weaken the bond between husband and wife and open spiritual doors.

2. CONFUSION IN CHILDREN

Identity confusion, peer pressure, and moral instability are spiritual attacks aimed at crippling the next generation.

3. BUSYNESS AND DISTRACTION

Satan doesn't need to make us evil, **only busy**. A distracted home becomes spiritually weak.

4. TEMPTATION AND SECRET SIN

Addictions, pornography, and emotional bonds outside the marriage weaken the spiritual covering of the home.

5. PULLING CHILDREN AWAY FROM PARENTS

Children outside the protective umbrella of parental authority become vulnerable to destructive influences. Outsiders become their main influence, the streets become their teacher, that is why I'm calling fathers, parents, grandparents, FIGHT FOR THEM ON YOUR KNEES AND ASK GOD TO GIVE YOU THE WISDOM AND INSIGHT IN WHAT YOU NEED TO HELP THEM. Prevention is much better than intervention.

6. FATHERLESSNESS

When fathers are weakened or absent, children suffer emotional, spiritual, and moral instability.

7. INVERTED PRIORITIES

When work, ministry, entertainment, or social acceptance come before family, **the home slowly collapses.**

PARENTS ARE THE PRIMARY TARGET

Discouraged parents lead to discouraged children. A divided marriage **destabilizes the next generation.**

THE ENEMY FEARS FAMILIES THAT SERVE THE LORD

A home that declares, **"As for me and my house, we will serve the Lord,"** becomes a fortress, a sanctuary, and a threat to darkness.

THE GOOD NEWS: The enemy CAN BE DEFEATED IN THE HOME

When families restore prayer, rebuild unity, forgive past wounds, remove ungodly influences, and return to God's order, the enemy loses his influence. Bring a Bible study into your home and pray together. Jesus asked His disciples to pray for an hour, yet they were sleeping and missed a great opportunity, as many homes do today. GOD ANSWERS PRAYER, AND I WILL SAY IT AGAIN "GOD ANSWERS PRAYERS."

A PRAYER OF PROTECTION

"Lord, protect our homes. Restore unity, heal wounds, and close every door the enemy has used. Fill our families with Your presence and surround us with Your protection. Help us to study your word and lead us to a good church where we can grow spiritually, In Jesus' name, Amen."

Hebrews 10:25 (English Standard Version): 25 not neglecting to meet together, as is the habit of some, but encouraging one another, and all the more as you see the Day drawing near.

CHAPTER FIVE: GOD FIRST— THE UNSHAKABLE FOUNDATION OF EVERY HOME

Every strong structure has a strong foundation. A family is no different. Jesus gave us a divine order for life: **God first, everything else second.**

Matthew 6:33 teaches us: "Seek first the kingdom of God and His righteousness, and all these things shall be added unto you." God is not asking to be important,He is asking to be first, **because nothing works unless He is the foundation.**

WHEN GOD IS NOT FIRST, EVERYTHING SHAKES

Marriages shake. Children drift. Finances collapse. Emotions grow unstable. A home **without God becomes spiritually unprotected.**

Only the presence of God can sustain a family.

GOD FIRST MEANS GOD'S WILL FIRST

Putting God first means:

- His Word above feelings
- His will above desires
- His voice above our own
- His truth above culture

- His presence above comfort

When God is first, the atmosphere of the home changes.

THE HEART OF THE FAMILY MUST TURN TOWARD GOD

A family that seeks God finds unity, healing, strength, and protection. God becomes the peace, the wisdom, and the light of the home.

PARENTS LEAD THE WAY

Children follow the example of their parents. **A father who prays is a shield. A mother who seeks God is a covering.** A home led by godly parents becomes a home with destiny.

GOD FIRST MEANS SURRENDER

We must surrender pride, ambition, money, entertainment, and busyness, **anything that sits on the throne of the heart before God.**

A HOME WITHOUT GOD BECOMES A BATTLEFIELD

Arguments increase, temptation grows, confusion rises, priorities shift, and the enemy gains easy access.

A HOME WITH GOD BECOMES A SANCTUARY

Peace, unity, clarity, love, forgiveness, and blessing flow. A sanctuary is any place where God dwells; **your home can become that place.**

A PRAYER FOR HOMES RETURNING TO GOD

"Heavenly Father, today we put You first again. Enter our home, restore unity, and fill every room with Your peace. We surrender our priorities and declare You are first above all things. Holy Spirit you are welcome into our home, and let your angels encamp around us we pray,In Jesus' name, Amen."

CHAPTER SIX: FAMILY SECOND—HONORING THE MOST PRECIOUS GIFT GOD GAVE YOU

After God, the greatest gift He has placed in your life is your family. Not your career, not ministry, not reputation—your family is God's treasure entrusted to your care.

FAMILY IS GOD'S ORDER

God first. Family second. Not because family is less important, but because everything else collapses when the home is neglected.

NEGLECTING THE FAMILY IS NEGLECTING GOD'S GIFT

People pray for blessings while ignoring the blessing they already have at home. **Your family is not a distraction from your calling, it is part of your calling.**

WHAT WILL GOD ASK YOU?

Not "How successful were you?" but "What did you do with the family I gave you? Did you love them, lead them, teach them, protect them?"

A LESSON FROM EXPERIENCE

You learned the pain of neglect. My first two boys were affected, distance formed, but restoration came because I fought for them. Neglect wounds, but God restores.

YOUR FIRST MINISTRY IS YOUR FAMILY

1 Timothy 3:4–5 teaches that if a person cannot care for their own home, they cannot care for God's work. **A ministry that destroys the family is not a ministry God blesses.**

CHILDREN DO NOT NEED PERFECT PARENTS, THEY NEED PRESENT PARENTS

Presence heals what words cannot. Children forgive failure more easily than absence.

THE FAMILY REFLECTS GOD'S HEART

Your love reflects Christ's love. Your leadership reflects God's leadership. Your unity reflects God's unity. Family is God's classroom to reveal His character.

FAMILY SECOND, BECAUSE IT STRENGTHENS EVERYTHING ELSE

A strong family strengthens work, ministry, faith, and purpose. You can rebuild a career, but you cannot replace a spouse or a child.

A PRAYER FOR STRENGTHENING THE HOME

"Father, thank You for the gift of family. Forgive us when we put other things above our home. Heal, restore, and strengthen every relationship. Let our homes reflect Your heart. In Jesus' name, Amen."

CHAPTER SEVEN: WORK THIRD, THE BLESSING OF PROVIDING WITHOUT LOSING YOUR HOME

Work is a blessing from God. Before sin entered the world, before struggle existed, God gave humanity the gift of work. Genesis 2:15 teaches us that God placed man in the garden "to tend it and keep it." Work teaches responsibility, stewardship, discipline, and purpose.

WORK IS HOLY, BUT NOT ABOVE YOUR FAMILY

Work becomes an idol when it takes more of your heart than God and more of your time than your family. Work is meant to support the home, not replace it. **Many marriages and relationships crumble because careers consume the energy and attention that families desperately need.**

THE BIBLE HONORS HARD WORK

Proverbs 12:11 and Proverbs 14:23 affirm the value of labor. Ephesians 4:28 teaches us to work so that we may provide for others. But Scripture also warns in 1 Timothy 5:8 that failing to care for our household is denying the faith. Providing is not only financial; it includes time, presence, love, and guidance.

WORK IS A BLESSING, NOT A BURDEN

Work becomes a burden when it steals identity, drains emotional strength, and robs the family of **meaningful connection**. Children grow up hearing, "Not today," "I'm busy," or "Maybe tomorrow," until tomorrow becomes years of missed memories.

After all I have gone through in life I now understand the importance of connecting with my boys and with my wonderful wife, what it means is this, we stop talking about ourselves and talk about them, lean in to where they are at, feel their joy, their emotions, their fears and shares the ups and downs of their lives. If your kids want you to watch a soccer game, or they want to show you something they are interested in, DO NOT walk away, that is your opportunity to CONNECT with them, that is the LOVE LANGUAGE they understand, my Dad cares, my Mom cares, they are interested in what I'm interested in, when you do that, you have become the parent they can be proud of to their friends.

YOUR FAMILY SHOULD NOT PAY THE PRICE FOR YOUR WORK

Workplaces replace people quickly, but families do not. Work should never receive your best while your spouse and children receive only your leftovers. **True provision includes emotional and spiritual presence.**

WHEN WORK IS THIRD, EVERYTHING BECOMES HEALTHIER

Placing work in its proper order brings peace, balance, clarity, and blessing. You become more productive, more focused, and more fulfilled when your priorities align with God's design. Remember you are NOT married to your work, your church, but to your family, that is why it is on top of the list. When we place things before them, families begin to crumble.

WORK HARD, BUT COME HOME WHOLE

Give your best at work, but bring your heart home. Bring your joy, attention, energy, and presence. Your family deserves the best of you—not what is left of you.

A PRAYER FOR BALANCE AND BLESSING

"Lord, thank You for the gift of work. Help me to honor You in all I do, without placing work above You or my family. Bring balance, blessing, and order to my life. In Jesus' name, Amen."

CHAPTER EIGHT: THE CHURCH, A PLACE OF STRENGTH, COMMUNITY & SPIRITUAL COVERING

The family is God's first institution, but the church is His spiritual home for His people. Hebrews 10:25 commands us not to forsake gathering together because the church strengthens, protects, and equips the home.

THE CHURCH IS A SPIRITUAL COVERING

When believers gather:

- Faith grows
- Marriages strengthen
- Children receive godly influence
- Homes gain spiritual protection
- Purpose becomes clearer

There are breakthroughs and spiritual battles we cannot face alone. God designed the church to be a shield around the family.

CHURCH IS NOT OPTIONAL, IT IS ESSENTIAL

The church is where:

- Truth is preached

- Worship transforms
- The Holy Spirit moves
- Children learn Scripture
- Fellowship strengthens faith
- Gifts are activated
- Destiny is revealed

Avoiding church weakens prayer, unity, convictions, accountability, and spiritual strength.

We face, in these last days, disappointments about what we see in churches today, but you are not there for individuals but for God. Find a church where you can all grow and where God is, where prayer is taught, a church that is not afraid to preach against sin, a place where your kids can grow spiritually, but above all, you are their parents.

THE CHURCH STRENGTHENS MARRIAGES

Healthy churches encourage men to lead, women to thrive, and couples to grow. Mentors, prayer, and wisdom strengthen marriages and provide support through storms.

THE CHURCH STRENGTHENS CHILDREN

Children face confusion, pressure, and spiritual attacks. A child raised in church gains truth, identity, godly friendships, and strength to resist temptation. I'm so grateful that my three boys belong to God. They are strong Christians, and I feel confident that the world they are facing now and the world they will face later are well within their reach because of their relationship with God.

THE MISTAKE MANY PARENTS MAKE

Sports, entertainment, and activities often replace church. This teaches children that God is optional. **Children will not value what their parents treat as non-essential. We MUST do it for them. I hear many teens who struggle a lot, and I see them hurting, or even in prison, because of broken homes or homes without a parent present or without God.**

Psalm 14:1-3 (New King James Version) Folly of the Godless *14 The fool has said in his heart, "There is no God."*

They are corrupt; they have done abominable works; there is none who does good.

*2 The Lord looks down from heaven upon the children of men, To see if there are any who understand, **who seek God.***

*3 They have all turned aside, They have together become corrupt; **There is none who does good, No, not one.***

CHURCH DOES NOT REPLACE THE HOME, IT EMPOWERS IT

The church reinforces what God builds in the home. **A strong church produces strong families, and strong families produce strong churches.**

DO NOT LET HURT PUSH YOU AWAY

Churches are filled with imperfect people seeking God. Hurt and offense are tools the enemy uses to isolate believers. Healing comes by reconnecting, not withdrawing.

I heard this story years ago, a woman was asked by a child to go to church, and she answered, TOO MANY HIPOCRATES THERE, the child answered and said, "I RATHER GO TO CHURCH AND BE AROUND A FEW HIPOCRATES, THAN SPEND ETERNITY WITH ALL OF THEM." ☺

A PRAYER FOR EVERY FAMILY IN GOD'S HOUSE

"Lord, thank You for the gift of Your church. Strengthen our commitment to gather and grow. Bless our pastors, our spiritual family, and our home. In Jesus' name, Amen."

CHAPTER NINE: MINISTRY LAST, BECAUSE IT IS THE MOST IMPORTANT ONE

Ministry is last in God's order, not because it is least important, but because it collapses if God, family, church, and work are not in alignment. Many believers put ministry above their homes, **but God never asked anyone to lose their family to serve Him**.

MINISTRY BEGINS AT HOME

Your first ministry is:

- Loving your spouse
- Leading your children
- Walking in integrity
- Building a home filled with God's presence

1 Timothy 3:4–5 teaches that if a person cannot lead their home, they cannot lead God's church. Ministry requires a strong foundation—**and that foundation is your family.**

MINISTRY WITHOUT ORDER BECOMES A BURDEN

Many become exhausted in ministry because they are carrying a weight God never intended for them to bear. They give their best to others, but their families receive the leftovers. This

imbalance destroys marriages, wounds children, and weakens the
home. It happened to me, I burned out many times, I was serving
God to impress Him, but neglecting my family. Once I learned
these principles, I DO NOT burn out anymore, I must do ONLY
what God requires of me.

YOUR MOST IMPORTANT DISCIPLES ARE YOUR CHILDREN

Before you preach or serve, you must shepherd your home.
Your marriage is your message. Your children are your disciples.
Your home is your pulpit. I see many Pastors neglecting their
families, and they paid a high price because of it, their children
away from God, in prison, in drugs, in wrong, ungodly
relationships, and some even commit suicide, all for the praise of
the people. God first, then is your family, the family God gave
you. For years, my identity in ministry was serving Him in
ministry. When I learned these principles, I realized that ministry
doesn't matter to me as it did before.

Matthew 22:37-40 (New King James Version): *37 Jesus said
to him, "'You shall love the Lord your God with all your heart,
with all your soul, and with all your mind.' 38 This is the first
and great commandment. 39 And the second is like it: 'You shall
love your neighbor as yourself.' 40 On these two commandments
hang all the Law and the Prophets."*

THE TRAGEDY OF NEGLECTING FAMILY FOR MINISTRY

Many pastors and leaders lose their children while saving others. Neglect leaves emotional wounds that the enemy uses to his advantage. **A child who feels replaced by ministry often feels rejected by God.**

MINISTRY FLOURISHES WHEN THE HOME IS STRONG

A strong marriage brings fresh anointing. Loved children bring stability. Aligned priorities bring blessing. Ministry grows when the home is healthy, not when the home is sacrificed.

MINISTRY IS LAST BECAUSE IT MUST REST ON A STRONG FOUNDATION

Ministry requires sacrifice, maturity, and stability. When God first, family second, and work third are in place, ministry becomes powerful and fruitful.

"MINISTRY IS NOT LAST BECAUSE IT IS THE LEAST, BUT BECAUSE IT IS WHERE WE ARE TOUCHING PEOPLE, HELPING PEOPLE." IF EVERYTHING IS IN PLACE, THEN WE WILL BE VERY EFFECTIVE IN WHAT WE DO.

A PRAYER FOR THOSE IN MINISTRY

"Lord, help me honor Your order. Strengthen my home, restore balance, and protect my family. Let my ministry flow from a place of health and blessing. In Jesus' name, Amen."

CHAPTER TEN: FORGIVENESS, HEALING & RESTORATION IN THE FAMILY

Forgiveness is the foundation of healing. Colossians 3:13 calls us to forgive as the Lord forgave us. Homes cannot heal without forgiveness, and families cannot be restored unless someone chooses to release the pain and surrender it to God.

FAMILIES BREAK WHERE FORGIVENESS IS MISSING

Every family experiences conflict, disappointment, and wounds. What destroys families is not conflict, but unresolved conflict. Unforgiveness creates bitterness, silence, division, and emotional walls that give the enemy access to the home.

FORGIVENESS DOES NOT EXCUSE THE OFFENSE, IT RELEASES THE HEART

Forgiveness is not approving what happened or pretending it didn't hurt. Forgiveness means releasing bitterness, giving the pain to God, and closing the door to the enemy. It brings freedom to the one who forgives.

HEALING BEGINS WHEN SOMEONE FORGIVES FIRST

Healing requires humility. Someone must choose to forgive first, whether spouse, parent, or child. Forgiveness is leadership. It is maturity. It is obedience to God.

FORGIVENESS RESTORES MARRIAGES

Many marriages die not from lack of love, but from lack of forgiveness. Forgiveness restores trust, communication, unity, intimacy, and peace.

FORGIVENESS HEALS CHILDREN AND PARENTS

Children carry wounds, harsh words, broken promises, and emotional distance. Parents also carry wounds, rejection, disrespect, and guilt. Forgiveness bridges the gap and restores broken years. Your own testimony of reconciling with your sons reflects this truth.

FORGIVENESS BREAKS GENERATIONAL CURSES

Homes that do not forgive pass down anger, bitterness, and emotional coldness. But forgiveness transforms the atmosphere and heals generations.

HEALING IS A PROCESS

Healing happens in steps:

1. Forgive
2. Give the pain to God
3. Rebuild communication
4. Rebuild trust slowly
5. Create new patterns
6. Invite God into the relationship

YOUR HOME CAN BECOME A PLACE OF RESTORATION

Forgiveness does not change the past—but it transforms the future. A home built on forgiveness becomes a place of love, safety, and healing.

A PRAYER FOR RESTORATION

"Father, teach us to forgive **as You forgave us.** Heal our wounds, restore our unity, and bring peace to our home. Let our family become a place of love and mercy. In Jesus' name, Amen."

CHAPTER ELEVEN: PRAYER IN THE HOME, THE SPIRITUAL COVERING THAT PROTECTS THE FAMILY

Prayer is the lifeline of the home. It is the shield of the family, the weapon of parents, and the spiritual atmosphere that invites God into every room. A home without prayer is spiritually unprotected, **but a home that prays becomes a fortress**.

PRAYER IS A COVERING THE ENEMY CANNOT PENETRATE

When a family prays:

- Peace fills the home
- Darkness is pushed out
- Angels are assigned
- Hearts soften
- God's presence rests there

A praying home denies the enemy access.

A PRAYING PARENT IS A SPIRITUAL WARRIOR

Parents who pray become protectors over their children. Your prayers go where you cannot—into schools, friendships, decisions, and future battles. Children may ignore words, **but they cannot outrun prayers.**

THE ENEMY FEARS HOMES THAT PRAY TOGETHER

A praying family is dangerous to darkness. The enemy cannot divide a home that prays, cannot confuse children covered in prayer, and cannot destroy a marriage that bows before God. A home in chaos is a home neglecting the power of Prayer. You see prayers brings the light of God unto us, and shines in us, reveals the right and the wrong, the right that confirms your good standing with God, but the wrong that you are NOT, and that is why people neglect praying, they do not want to see their darkness, or their idols that keeps them blind to the things of God, I have a saying, "DO NOT COMPLAIN FOR WHAT YOU HAVE ALLOWED."

PRAYER MUST BECOME DAILY IN THE HOME

Prayer is not a last resort, **it is a first priority**. Families should pray in the morning, before meals, before bed, in conflict, and in celebration. Short prayers matter. Consistency matters more.

Psalm 63:1-8 (New King James Version): Joy in the Fellowship of God. A Psalm of David when he was in the wilderness of Judah.

63 O God, You are my God;

Early will I seek You;

My soul thirsts for You;

My flesh longs for You

In a dry and thirsty land

Where there is no water.

2 So I have looked for You in the sanctuary,

To see Your power and Your glory.

3 Because Your lovingkindness is better than life,

My lips shall praise You.

4 Thus I will bless You while I live;

I will lift up my hands in Your name.

5 My soul shall be satisfied as with [a]marrow and [b]fatness,

And my mouth shall praise You with joyful lips.

6 When I remember You on my bed,

I meditate on You in the night watches.

7 Because You have been my help,

Therefore in the shadow of Your wings I will rejoice.

8 My soul follows close behind You;

Your right hand upholds me.

CHILDREN NEED TO HEAR THEIR PARENTS PRAY

Prayer shapes identity. Hearing their parents pray teaches children how to trust God, worship Him, and fight spiritual battles. **They may forget sermons, but they never forget a praying father or mother.**

PRAYER BRINGS BREAKTHROUGHS, PARENTS CANNOT

Some battles parents cannot fix—rebellion, fear, addiction, emotional wounds. But prayer reaches into places human hands cannot touch. Many victories in a child's life are won through unseen prayers. It also brings healing from illnesses affecting the family. We, as a family, have experienced His healing power many times, and still, NOW we know He is a Healer, a great God, and He gives His children gifts in many forms.

My boys saw me a couple of times, one was near death, and the other had stage 2 cancer of the prostate. They saw faith in God, they saw us trusting God, and they saw us HEALED from those physical challenges. So one day, when they are experiencing similar situations in their lives or in their families', they can apply what they saw and see God move on their behalf and heal them. God still heals today.

PRAYER BRINGS UNITY INTO THE MARRIAGE

Prayer heals, restores, calms, softens, and connects. Couples who pray together remain spiritually united. **A marriage built on prayer becomes unbreakable.**

MAKE YOUR HOME A PLACE OF PRAYER

Choose a time, choose a place, and invite God into your home daily. A praying house may not be perfect, but it will be protected.

A PRAYER TO RESTORE PRAYER IN THE HOME

"Lord, make our home a house of prayer. Cover our family with Your presence. Strengthen us in every battle, unite us in love, and let peace fill every room. In Jesus' name, Amen."

CHAPTER TWELVE: TEACHING MORALS, VALUES & GODLY CHARACTER TO THE NEXT GENERATION

A nation stands or falls based on the morals and values of its people. A home is strengthened or weakened by the character taught within it. God commands parents to intentionally shape the next generation, not leaving their development to the world.

THE CRISIS OF TODAY: A GENERATION WITHOUT MORAL DIRECTION

Children today are disciplined more by culture than by parents. Influencers, celebrities, music, social media, and peers often hold more influence than godly role models. The world teaches rebellion, confusion, pride, and immorality—never respect, purity, or godliness.

Unless parents teach values, the world will teach its own version, and its version destroys.

GOD COMMANDS PARENTS TO TEACH VALUES DAILY

Deuteronomy 6:7 instructs parents to teach God's ways continually. Moral education must be intentional, consistent, and rooted in Scripture. Schools, friends, or society cannot replace a parent's responsibility.

GODLY CHARACTER DOES NOT HAPPEN AUTOMATICALLY

Character must be trained and modeled. **Children become what they see.**

ESSENTIAL GODLY CHARACTER TRAITS

- Honesty
- Respect
- Humility
- Self-control
- Purity
- Obedience
- Responsibility
- Compassion
- Courage
- Faithfulness
- Fear of the Lord

These traits shape leaders, build strong families, and strengthen nations.

PARENTS MUST MODEL WHAT THEY WANT TO SEE

Children imitate actions, not instructions. Parents must live the values they want their children to have—truth, forgiveness, purity, prayer, humility, and integrity.

FIVE WAYS TO BUILD GODLY CHARACTER IN CHILDREN

1. Teach Scripture regularly
2. Build daily habits of prayer
3. Set clear boundaries and consequences
4. Shepherd the heart, not just behavior
5. Celebrate and affirm godly choices

WITHOUT VALUES, HOMES BREAK—WITH VALUES, HOMES THRIVE

When morals disappear, families fall apart. When values are taught, children feel secure, marriages strengthen, communities improve, and nations rise.

A PRAYER FOR PARENTS

"Lord, help us teach our children Your ways. Strengthen us to model godly character and protect our children from the influence of the world. Make our home a place of righteousness. In Jesus' name, Amen."

CHAPTER THIRTEEN: RESTORING THE FAMILY ALTAR, BRINGING GOD BACK INTO THE HOME

There was a time when families gathered to read Scripture, pray, and worship together. This place of devotion and unity was known as the family altar. **As this altar disappeared, so did much of the home's spiritual strength.**

WHAT IS THE FAMILY ALTAR?

The family altar is not furniture—it is a moment where the family seeks God together. It is:

- A time of prayer
- A place of Scripture
- A space for worship
- A moment of teaching and blessing
- A covering over the home

WHERE THERE IS NO ALTAR, THE HOME IS UNPROTECTED

Without prayer and God's presence:

- Arguments increase

- Confusion grows
- Children drift
- Marriages weaken
- The enemy gains access

When the altar is restored:

- Peace returns
- Unity strengthens
- Hearts soften
- Children feel secure
- God's presence fills the home

WHAT HAPPENS AT THE FAMILY ALTAR?

- Reading Scripture
- Praying together
- Worshiping together
- Speaking blessings
- Sharing testimonies
- Listening to each other's hearts

ELIJAH RESTORED THE ALTAR BEFORE REVIVAL CAME

1 Kings 18:30 — *"Elijah repaired the altar of the LORD that had been torn down."*

After the altar was restored, God moved with fire. When you restore the altar in your home, **God restores the home itself.**

WHY CHILDREN NEED A FAMILY ALTAR

It teaches them:

- How to pray
- How to know God
- How to hear His voice
- How to stand in storms
- How to walk in purity and truth

WHY MARRIAGES NEED A FAMILY ALTAR

A praying marriage:

- Heals faster
- Forgives easier
- Discerns spiritually
- Builds intimacy
- Walks in unity
- Overcomes temptation

HOW TO RESTORE THE ALTAR

1. Choose a time
2. Keep it simple
3. Make it regular
4. Remove distractions
5. Lead with love
6. Let children participate
7. Be patient

WHEN GOD RETURNS TO THE CENTER, EVERYTHING FALLS INTO PLACE

A home with an altar experiences peace, protection, breakthrough, unity, restoration, and spiritual growth.

A PRAYER TO RESTORE THE FAMILY ALTAR

"Lord, we rebuild the altar in our home. Fill this house with Your presence. Teach us to seek You daily, worship together, and walk in Your ways. Restore our family through Your presence. In Jesus' name, Amen."

CHAPTER FOURTEEN: PROTECTING THE HOME FROM THE ENEMY'S ATTACKS

Your home is under attack because it has purpose. The enemy fears a godly marriage, a praying family, and children raised in truth. If he destroys the home, he destroys the nation. But God has given families authority and spiritual weapons to stand strong.

THE ENEMY ATTACKED THE FIRST FAMILY IN EDEN

Satan used deception, confusion, and division against Adam and Eve, the same strategies he uses today. He attacks communication, unity, trust, obedience, and spiritual discipline.

RECOGNIZING THE ENEMY'S FOOTSTEPS

You sense the enemy's activity when:

- Arguments increase
- Peace disappears
- Children drift
- Temptation intensifies
- Distractions dominate
- Prayer becomes difficult
- Emotional coldness grows

- Pride blocks communication
- Spiritual laziness enters

The enemy often enters through disconnection.

OPEN DOORS ALLOW ATTACKS

Doors that invite spiritual attacks include:

- Unforgiveness
- Anger
- Bitterness
- Pornography
- Addictions
- Wrong friendships
- Occult entertainment
- Sexual sin
- Passive spiritual leadership

When a door is open, the attack is legal. When it is closed, the attack is defeated.

PARENTS ARE SPIRITUAL GATEKEEPERS

Parents, especially fathers, must watch, guard, pray, discern, and protect. A home without a spiritual watchman becomes vulnerable.

FIVE WAYS TO PROTECT YOUR HOME

1. Pray over your home daily

2. Guard what enters your home

3. Remove every open door to the enemy

4. Speak blessings, not curses

5. Stay spiritually alert

WHY THE ENEMY FEARS A GOD-PROTECTED HOME

A godly home produces strong marriages, God-fearing children, spiritual leaders, generational blessings, and families that shape communities.

A PRAYER OF PROTECTION

"Lord, my home belongs to You. Expose every attack, close every door to darkness, and cover our family with Your blood and Your angels. No weapon formed against us will prosper. In Jesus' name, Amen."

CHAPTER FIFTEEN: THE STRENGTH OF A NATION BEGINS WITH THE STRENGTH OF ITS FAMILIES

Every nation searches for strength.

Governments look for it in policies.

Leaders look for it in power.

Economies look for it in wealth.

Armies look for it in weapons.

But God has always revealed a deeper truth:

The true strength of a nation is not found in its government—it is found in its families.

When families are strong, nations stand firm.

When families collapse, nations slowly crumble from within.

History proves this.

Scripture confirms this.

Society is living this reality today.

Nations Do Not Fall Suddenly — They Fall Gradually

A nation rarely collapses overnight.

It weakens slowly, quietly, almost invisibly.

First, morals decline.

Then marriages weaken.

Then children lose direction.

Then homes lose stability.

Then truth disappears.

Then confusion spreads.

Then the nation begins to fall.

The collapse of a nation is almost always the result of the collapse of the family. Because the family is the first school, the first government, the first church, and the first place where character is formed.

Destroy the family, and the nation has no future.

Strong Families Produce Strong Citizens

Every judge, teacher, pastor, police officer, leader, and president was first a child in a home.

What they become in public is shaped by what they experienced in private.

A child raised in:

- Love becomes an adult who values people.

- Discipline becomes an adult with responsibility.

- Prayer becomes an adult who seeks God.

- Truth becomes an adult with integrity.

- Respect becomes an adult who honors authority.

- Stability becomes an adult who builds, not destroys.

But a child raised in:

- Chaos

- Neglect

- Violence

- Moral confusion

- Fatherlessness

- Spiritual emptiness

often carries those wounds into society.

Society is simply a reflection of the condition of the home.

The Enemy Knows This — That's Why He Attacks Families First

Satan does not begin by attacking governments. He begins by attacking marriages. He targets children. He weakens fathers. He exhausts mothers. He divides homes. He removes prayer. He replaces truth with confusion.

Because he understands:

If he destroys the family today, he controls the nation tomorrow. This is why restoring families is not just a personal issue—it is a spiritual and national mission.

Revival in a Nation Begins in the Living Room

Many people pray for national revival. They look to churches, conferences, movements, and leaders. But God's pattern is different.

Revival does not begin on a stage.

Revival begins in a home.

When:

- Husbands return to loving their wives
- Wives return to honoring their husbands
- Parents return to discipling their children
- Families return to prayer
- Homes return to holiness
- God returns to the center

Then revival spreads outward—from the home to the church, to the community, to the nation.

The path to national restoration always passes through the family living room.

God's Design Has Never Changed

From the beginning, God built society on one foundation: The family.

Before governments existed…

before laws were written…

before nations were formed…

God created a man, a woman, and a home.

Because God knew:

If the family remains strong, the nation will remain stable.

His design has never changed—even if culture has.

The Responsibility of This Generation

Every generation decides whether the next generation will be stronger or weaker.

We must ask:

- Will we rebuild marriages?
- Will we protect children?
- Will we restore prayer in the home?
- Will we teach truth again?
- Will we honor God's design for family?

Because if we do…our children will inherit strength.

If we do not…they will inherit confusion.

The future of a nation is being decided right now inside ordinary homes.

What Happens When Families Become Strong Again

When families return to God's order:

- Crime decreases
- Communities stabilize
- Schools improve
- Churches grow stronger
- Leaders rise with integrity
- Economies become healthier
- Hope returns
- Nations are renewed

Because strong families create strong futures.

No political program can replace what a godly home produces.

The Call to Rebuild the Family

This book is more than teaching.

It is a call.

A call to fathers to rise again.

A call to mothers to stand strong.

A call to marriages to heal.

A call to children to return home.

A call to families to pray again.

A call to place God first again.

Because rebuilding the family is the first step to rebuilding the nation. And the responsibility does not belong to governments—it belongs to us.

A Vision of Hope

The story of the family is not finished.

Broken homes can be healed.

Lost children can return.

Marriages can be restored.

Prayer can return to living rooms.

God can return to the center.

And when families rise again…nations will rise with them.

A PRAYER FOR THE RESTORATION OF FAMILIES AND NATIONS

Heavenly Father,

We ask You to restore the family in our generation. Heal marriages, protect children, strengthen parents, and bring Your presence back into our homes. Let strong families rise in every city and every nation. Let truth return, let prayer return, let holiness return. And through restored families, bring healing to the nations of the world.

We declare that the future will be stronger because families are returning to You.

In Jesus' name,

Amen.

CHAPTER SIXTEEN: FINANCIAL WISDOM, HOW MONEY CAN DESTROY OR STRENGTHEN A FAMILY

If there is one topic that destroys more marriages, divides more homes, and wounds more children than almost anything else, it is finances.

Not money itself—but the mismanagement of money, the secrecy around money, the arguments about money, and the stress caused by financial disorder.

Scripture never says money is evil.

It says:

"The LOVE of money is the root of all evil."— 1 Timothy 6:10

Money is not the problem.

The heart behind how we use money is the problem.

A family that handles finances wisely becomes strong, stable, peaceful, and prosperous.

A family that handles finances poorly becomes stressed, divided, resentful, and spiritually vulnerable.

Finances can either destroy a home—or build a generational blessing.

WHEN FINANCES ARE OUT OF ORDER, THE HOME FALLS APART

Most marriages today are not destroyed by infidelity, abuse, or personality differences.

Most marriages are destroyed by:

- Financial stress
- Debt
- Overspending
- Poor priorities
- Secrets between husband and wife
- Lack of budgeting
- Irresponsibility
- Pressure to maintain an image
- Greed
- Poor credit
- Fear of lack

When money is mishandled, the atmosphere of the home changes:

- Peace leaves
- Arguments increase

- Patience disappears
- Blame becomes normal
- Trust weakens
- Children feel the tension

Financial stress affects love, communication, emotional intimacy, and spiritual unity.

Where there is no financial order, there is no peace.

Honesty in Finances Is a Biblical Requirement

A marriage cannot survive financial lies.

Husbands and wives weaken their covenant when they:

- Hide purchases
- Hide accounts
- Hide debt
- Hide credit card usage
- Hide financial struggles
- Hide income
- Hide financial mistakes

Secrets destroy trust. And trust is one of the pillars of marriage.

Amos 3:3 asks: *"Can two walk together unless they agree?"*

A husband and wife must walk in:

- Agreement

- Transparency

- Honesty

- Communication

- Shared goals

- Shared priorities

Financial honesty protects the marriage covenant.

PARENTS MUST BECOME A TEMPLATE FOR THEIR CHILDREN

Children observe everything.

If parents:

- Fight about money

- Overspend

- Live in debt

- Misuse credit

- Lack financial discipline

- Refuse to tithe

- Complain about bills

- Make impulsive decisions

The children will repeat the same cycle as adults.

But if parents model:

- Wisdom
- Discipline
- Generosity
- Delayed gratification
- Stewardship
- Gratitude
- Saving
- Budgeting
- Financial honesty

—the children will grow into adults who know how to manage their finances and honor God.

Your example becomes their financial DNA.

Teaching Children About Finances Is a Biblical Principle

Proverbs 22:6 says: *"Train up a child in the way he should go…"*

Children must learn:

- How to earn money
- How to save money
- How to spend wisely
- How to avoid debt
- How to build credit
- How to manage responsibility

- How to give to God
- How to live below their means
- How to steward blessings
- How to honor God with their increase

A child who grows up with financial discipline becomes an adult who prospers.

This is why so many families suffer today—parents never taught their children financial wisdom, and now entire generations repeat the same financial mistakes.

A Good Credit Score Is Not Just Practical—It Is Spiritual Wisdom.

Credit affects:

- Housing
- Interest rates
- Car payments
- Job opportunities
- Insurance
- Financial freedom
- Stress levels
- Adult life stability

Parents who teach their children the importance of good credit are giving them:

- Stability

- Opportunity

- Protection

- Discipline

- A future free of unnecessary struggle

A good name is valuable.

A good reputation matters.

A good credit score is part of being a responsible steward.

Proverbs 22:1 says: *"A good name is more desirable than great riches."*

Financial integrity is part of a good name.

TITHING—GIVING TO GOD WHAT BELONGS TO HIM

No financial teaching is complete without this truth:

All blessing comes from God.

Every paycheck.

Every opportunity.

Every open door.

Every promotion.

Every increase.

We give to God because He is the source of everything we have.

Malachi 3:10 says: *"Bring all the tithe into the storehouse… and I will open the windows of heaven."*

Tithing is:

- Obedience
- Trust
- Honor
- Worship
- A reminder that money is not our god

Families who tithe experience:

- Supernatural provision
- Peace in finances
- Protection from devourers
- Unexpected blessings
- Financial wisdom
- Divine increase

When parents model generosity, children learn that God is the source, not the bank account.

A Family That Honors God With Its Finances Will Lack Nothing.

David declared: *"I have never seen the righteous forsaken nor their children begging for bread."* — Psalm 37:25

When parents:

- Walk in honesty
- Guard their finances
- Teach wisdom
- Live with discipline
- Maintain good credit
- Avoid debt
- Practice generosity
- Tithe faithfully
- Trust God
- Model stewardship

Their children:

- Prosper
- Avoid unnecessary struggles
- Learn responsibility
- Build generational wealth
- Avoid the traps of the world
- Grow with confidence
- Live with peace
- Become financially stable adults

Financial wisdom does not just bless parents—it blesses generations.

A FAMILY BUILT ON FINANCIAL INTEGRITY BECOMES A FAMILY GOD CAN PROSPER

God cannot bless disorder.

God cannot bless dishonesty.

God cannot bless irresponsibility.

God cannot bless selfishness.

But God WILL bless:

- Order
- Integrity
- Unity
- Stewardship
- Generosity
- Tithing
- Sacrifice
- Faithfulness

A financially honest, generous, disciplined home becomes a magnet for God's blessing.

Such a home will never lack what it needs, and its children will walk into adulthood with stability, wisdom, and divine favor.

A PRAYER FOR FINANCIAL WISDOM & BLESSING IN THE HOME

"Heavenly Father, Teach our family to honor You with our finances. Give us wisdom, discipline, honesty, and stewardship. Close every door of financial destruction. Heal the wounds caused by financial stress. Unite us in purpose and responsibility. Bless our efforts and guide our decisions. Let our children prosper because of the foundation we build today. We declare that every blessing comes from You and we choose to honor You with what You have given us. In Jesus' name, Amen."

CONCLUSION: A LEGACY THAT WILL BLESS GENERATIONS

This book began with a simple but eternal truth:

The strength of a nation is found in the strength of its families.

Not in politics.

Not in wealth.

Not in power.

But in homes where God is honored, marriages are protected, children are loved, and truth is lived daily.

Across these chapters, we have seen that God's order for life is clear:

- God first.
- Family second.
- Work third.
- Church as covering.
- Ministry flowing from a healthy home.

When this order is broken, families weaken.

When families weaken, nations drift.

But when this order is restored, everything begins to heal—from the living room outward to the world.

We have spoken about marriage, children, prayer, forgiveness, finances, spiritual protection, moral character, and restoring the family altar.

Each one is not just a teaching—it is a pathway back to strength.

Because God has never abandoned the family. And the future is not lost.

Broken marriages can be restored.

Wounded children can be healed.

Homes without prayer can become houses of God again.

Financial struggles can become testimonies of provision.

Generational pain can become generational blessing.

Restoration is possible.

Hope is alive.

God is still rebuilding families.

And when families rise again…nations will rise with them.

THE RESPONSIBILITY NOW BELONGS TO US

This message is not only to be read. It is to be lived.

The future of your children…

the future of your community…

the future of your nation…Is being shaped right now inside ordinary homes.

Every prayer you pray, every act of forgiveness, every moment you choose love, every sacrifice you make for your family—is building a legacy that will outlive you.

You may never stand before a nation, but if you build a godly family, you will shape the future of a nation.

ONE FINAL CALL

Return to God.

Restore the altar.

Protect the marriage.

Teach the children.

Honor His order.

Live in truth.

Walk in love.

Pray without ceasing.

Because the greatest revival of our time will not begin in stadiums or governments—it will begin in the family. And it can begin in your home today.

FINAL PRAYER

Heavenly Father, Thank You for the gift of family. Strengthen every home that reads these words. Restore what has been broken, heal what has been wounded, and bring Your presence back to the center of our lives.

Let strong families rise in every generation so that nations may be healed. We dedicate our homes, our marriages, our children, and our future to You.

In Jesus' name, Amen.